THE FEMININE ADVANTAGE

5 REASONS WHY WOMEN
MAKE GREAT REAL ESTATE INVESTORS

TAMMY RAGHUBIR & RAYMOND AARON

ISBN: 9781772770308

PUBLISHED BY:
10-10-10 PUBLISHING
MARKHAM, ON
CANADA

Dedication

*This book is dedicated to my daughter, Emily,
and to you, the readers, that you may find inspiration
to take action and invest wisely.*

Contents

Acknowledgements

I would like to take this opportunity to thank Raymond Aaron and his wonderful staff for all of their advice, patience and professionalism through this process of the creation of this book.

Our business partners Raymond and Alejandra, our real estate team players who are responsible for successfully handling our deals and advising us from pre-purchase to closing. I especially want to thank Monty Albert for all of his time and patience, coaching, and follow up telephone conversations, and for his valuable real estate agent referrals to my choice investment locations. I also would like to thank the real estate agents he referred me to, for all of their patience with my multitude of questions with potential properties, and for the extra mile they went for me.

Laure Ampilhac, for taking the time to allow me to interview her and agreeing to share her story with readers.

I also want to thank the authors of the books I have read, especially *Rich Dad*, and the Keyspire seminars I have attended that taught me ways of winning in real estate and creative deal structures, and by letting me know it is possible to begin investing in real estate with little money down.

Foreword

The Feminine Advantage is a must read for you working towards success in the field of real estate investing. For many years, women felt that this area of expertise was for MEN ONLY but no more. Many women like you, have come to realize that you have unique talents and abilities that make you perfectly suited to not only make money in real estate investing, but also have all the benefits that financial freedom can bring.

Tammy Raghubir and Raymond Aaron reveal in this book, the secrets to why you as a woman already have everything you need to thrive and succeed in the fast-paced world of real estate investing.

If you are just starting out, you will gain valuable advice that will help you miss some of the major pitfalls you would have faced. If you have been doing this for a while, you will find many ways to take your business further, faster. Each chapter contains practical steps that you can implement today and see results.

You will learn how your ability to multitask gives you a great advantage, plus how to use your naturally given, intuitive side to find the best properties for the best price.

If you have ever wondered about the role of relationships in real estate investing, look no further. Tammy will show you how to leverage the powerful dynamics of interrelationships to build a long-lasting business that brings in residual income like clockwork.

I urge you to read this book from cover to cover; it will be one of the best decisions you will ever make.

Loral Langemeier
New York Times Bestselling Author
of *The Millionaire Maker*

Your Journey Starts Here

Welcome to the journey of building wealth with real estate investment! I've written this book because I believe that women have an innate advantage as real estate investors, and I want to use what I've learned in my own journey with investing and in working with Raymond to empower you to take the plunge. You may be surprised to learn how close you already are to creating an income stream that supports your ideal lifestyle. I'm living proof that it's possible.

When I was laid off from my office job five years ago, I realized that I needed to take my future into my own hands, because there is no such thing as job security when you work for someone else. In my search for options that offered greater freedom and financial stability, I found like-minded people who shared similar investing goals through real estate seminars I attended. Attending these seminars brought life to the books I have read from the library relating to real estate investing.

I had then decided to surround myself with successful investors who weren't afraid to be bold. This was invaluable to me since the people around me did not offer such empowering examples for the most part. Talking with like-minded investors has given me access to connect with people that inspire me to dare to be different by taking well-informed risks that pay off well. In real estate, I realized I found a way to win four ways: cash flow after expenses, appreciation, forced appreciation, and by increasing net operating income (NOI). The most rewarding to me, is the less tangible value that I hold most dear: the time I get to spend raising my daughter, and not paying someone else to do it for me. As parents, that's time we can never get back.

Raymond is a very astute property investor and, when we compared notes on our journeys with real estate, we realized that *all* women are poised to achieve success as real estate investors. Whether you are a single professional looking to grow your retirement fund, or a parent seeking to provide a better life for your child, there are steps you can take today to build a real estate investment business that supports your long-term financial goals. You only need to get educated on the subject and begin building the network you'll need to help you take advantage of opportunities when they come.

Why do I believe that women are well-suited to real estate investment? It comes down to several skill areas in which we naturally excel, that work in favour of our investment efforts. Some examples of these include multi-tasking and management, intuition and a keen eye for detail, and *relationships and listening.* I emphasize these last two for a reason; few businesses depend more on a strong network than real estate, and women's natural talent for networking sets us up for success. Also, our inborn ability to judge character and read relationship dynamics gives us an advantage in our assessment of both potential investment partners and would-be tenants. When we listen to our gut on these matters, we are less likely to ally ourselves with the wrong people, thus avoiding some of the costly mistakes that commonly befall beginning real estate investors.

And, how many women do you know who *don't* love to shop? While shopping for real estate may carry higher stakes than hitting the clearance racks at your favourite department store, many of the same principles apply: there are always good deals if you know where to look, but if something doesn't fit it's not worth buying at any price. It's really the same exact thing in many ways, but on a bigger scale.

Now that I've given you a taste of what awaits you in the pages to come, I'm excited to begin! Raymond and I are ready to show you why you are already well-equipped to enter the world of real estate and build a thriving business for the benefit of you and your family. We hope this book empowers you to seize the opportunities that you're sure to discover, once you know where to look.

Yours Sincerely,
Tammy Raghubir

Chapter 1
Multitasking is in Our DNA

Unless you try to do something beyond what
you have already mastered, you will never grow.
— Ralph Waldo Emerson

The conventional wisdom has long been that women are natural at multi-tasking. If you happen to be a mother, you'll understand why. Raising children is a challenge that requires organization, patience, and a lot of consistency. This brings about opportunities to develop your skill in such a way that it becomes a naturally a part of you, and just when you accomplish your skills in that area and it becomes routine, they grow up to the next phase and present the next set of challenges that you need to re-organize and change your game plan to accommodate the new phase. There are always opportunities for growth, just like in real estate.

Every year, our responsibilities and tasks naturally increase, whether it be in the workplace, family home, around holiday time, and for special occasions. To accomplish these tasks successfully, we may naturally create a list as a way to keep organized.

Of course anyone can multi-task, and most people do to some degree, but doing it well is more rare. As women, we tend to reflect on an issue while juggling other tasks simultaneously. This is an advantage for entrepreneurs in any field, but it is particularly helpful in the world of real estate investment. There are so many factors to consider when choosing whether or not to purchase a property, and a complex series of steps must be followed once the choice is made.

From viewing properties and having them appraised, to applying for mortgages and setting up inspections, at each stage an investor must reflect on how all the pieces are fitting together for any potential addition to her portfolio. A woman's ability to perform several of these tasks simultaneously, while continually reflecting on the state of progress, allows her to stay on top of the real-estate investment game from start to finish.

Let's Get Real

Now let's be real for a moment. Perhaps you're already feeling overwhelmed just reading this, and you're wondering whether it applies to you and your over-busy, over-scheduled life. Believe me, I sympathize: as women, whether we work outside the home or not, it can seem as if some cruel law of nature conspires to fill every moment of our spare time with mundane tasks. Nature may abhor a vacuum, but not as much as our schedules do! When you finally get a moment to just sit down and grab a cup of tea, you may feel a twinge of disbelief. You know that soon enough, some new little crisis will explode on the scene, especially if you tempt fate by reaching for your favourite book or magazine.

In light of this, I understand why it might seem daunting to add such a complex adventure as real estate investment to your plate, no matter how motivated you might otherwise be. Lest you give up before you've started, however, consider this: once you begin your foray into real estate investing, the mundane tasks in your life can serve as moments of reflection, in which valuable insights can come to you. With practice, you can train yourself to make use of these moments in service of your real estate investing (REI) business.

How, you ask? Have you ever had the solution to a problem dawn on you while you were washing dishes or doing laundry? If you're a busy mom like I am, or a manager in charge of several projects at work, you may already have a system in place to help you keep track of those little insights that tend to float into your head when you least expect them. Just carrying a notebook and pen everywhere you go can be an invaluable tool to help you capture them, so you can go back and 'connect the dots' when you have the time.

If you're going to start your explorations of property investment on the side (whether you work outside the home or not – I believe that all moms are 'working' moms), then a good first step is to figure out how much time you can set aside each week for your new business.

If you're a stay-at-home mom with school-aged kids, you may be able to dedicate a good chunk of time right from the beginning to getting educated, doing research, and building your network. If you work full-time (or if your children are very young) you'll need to start smaller.

Because real estate investment is such a complex topic and can seem overwhelming when you're new to it, I recommend that you begin by simply deciding exactly how much time you wish to dedicate to your new venture on a daily, weekly, and monthly basis. This way, you'll be building it into the life you already have in a way that feels manageable. Remember that you won't make any progress if you take on too much, and it's not worth sacrificing your own well-being or that of your family in an effort to move too fast. While multi-tasking is inevitable, the old adages still apply: slow and steady wins the race, and if mom's not happy, nobody's happy!

When you're just starting out, you may wish to brainstorm all the things you're already aware of that may be involved in beginning your foray into real estate investment.

Make a list of everything you know you need to learn, and prioritize each area in a way that makes sense to you. Acknowledge which areas you already feel comfortable with (reading how-to books, networking and reviewing listings, for example), and which feel more challenging (legal aspects or building codes, perhaps).

If possible, look for ways that you can manage real estate-related tasks using the tools you already have in place for work and home. For example, you could join a local group for people exploring real estate investment and add their online calendar to your own, so you can see their events alongside your personal appointments. By making use of the organizational systems you already have, you'll make your first steps into the world of real estate investment fit seamlessly into your life.

On the following page are some examples of tasks that you might start with, and a sample schedule to give you an idea of how you can begin to fit these tasks into your life right now. This schedule assumes you work outside the home; if you're a homemaker, you might be able to condense many of the tasks on this schedule into one day, depending on the extent of your other commitments. If you start by determining how much time you want to devote to your real estate enterprise each day, week, and month, it should be easy to choose goals that feel manageable. Remember the wise words of Lao-Tse: *a journey of a thousand miles begins with a single step.*

Sample List of Tasks for Beginning Real Estate Investors:

- *Research educational opportunities for new real estate investors, both online and in person. This includes real estate investment blogs and online investor forums.*

- *Put the word out to your network that you're getting into real estate investment, and request help making potentially useful connections.*

- *Obtain and read books on real estate investment.*

- *Look into the possibility of working with a coach or forming an investment team — do you already know anyone who may be interested?*

Now, let's look at how you might fit these tasks into your current schedule:

	Morning	Lunch	Evening
Monday	Search Amazon and Library for good books on REI	Look for blogs and groups to join online	Pick up books from library or bookstore
Tuesday	Search for local or online courses on REI	Think about what kinds of properties I want to invest in, and why	Start reading books and taking notes
Wednesday	Keep reading and taking notes	Catch up on REI blogs	Schedule time for an in-depth talk with husband this weekend
Thursday	Put the word out on Facebook and LinkedIn that I'm getting into REI	Call someone in my network who I know is also interested in REI	Plan meeting with potential investment partners within the next month
Friday	More reading and taking notes	Refine to-dos based on what I've learned	Follow up on any networking leads

Chapter 2
We are Great at Keeping Our Eyes on the Prize

It is not because things are difficult that we dare not venture. It's
because we dare not venture that they are difficult.
– Lucius Annaeus Seneca

In the previous chapter, we looked at how women's natural talent for multi-tasking sets us up well to invest in real estate, whether we work outside the home or spend our days keeping a busy household running. Now, we're going to look at how that skill works together with another trait that is strong in many women: discernment.

Women are naturally drawn to look beneath the surface when faced with choices that affect ourselves, our loved ones, and the community as a whole. At a superficial level, we call this being *detail-oriented*. Whether we're decorating a room, meeting new people, managing a complex project, or house hunting, we intuitively understand that paying attention to the little things can mean the difference between a mediocre experience for all involved and an outstanding one. Our keen eye for detail allows us to hone in on subtle red flags when considering a property, like mouse poop or little piles of dust that can indicate the presence of termites.

At a deeper level, women usually listen when our intuition tells us to take a step back and reconsider a situation- I call this discernment. This commitment to reviewing our perceptions and assumptions allows us to view the situation neutrally, without the interference of our pre-conceived notions.The ability to discern is a very valuable skill when it comes to looking at a potential property. It is very easy to get emotional with respect to a property, and at times, you may find yourself in this state-of-mind, maybe because of a certain characteristic in the home that may catch your attention, and you might choose one property over the other based on an emotional decision. When it comes to investing in real estate, it is important to separate our emotions and focus on the numbers. When you are looking to purchase your principal residence, then house shopping with emotion will work out much better, rather than focusing on the numbers. It is important to remind yourself from time to time to make the switch between making an emotional decision, and investment decision.

Sometimes you may find a few good deals at the same time. I have encountered this many times. When I find myself in this situation, I was able to narrow it down by carefully going through my list of features I liked about each property, along with their respective location. My list also included a comparison of what the numbers looked like. In my opinion, the side-by-side comparison is a very effective method.

I have walked into a lot of homes. I am at the point in which as soon as I walk in, I am able to tell whether or not it is a good investment fairly quickly, without any number comparison. I don`t recommend you do this if you are just starting out, but after a while of going through the same process over and over, I found it easier to rely more on what I have gained through experience to be confident to move forward with my decision.

Focusing attention to detail applied to real estate is very valuable. From your first sighting of a property, to the initial conversation with the seller's agent, to your final walk-through and appraisal, your ability to synthesize a wealth of details into a clear picture enhances the likelihood that you'll get a good deal. When you connect the dots in this way, you're better able to ask the right questions to get to the truth about the cash flow potential of a given property.

Balancing Discernment and Opportunity

Canadian real estate investor and coach Laure Ampilhac is an excellent example of someone who knows how to balance discernment with seizing opportunity to build a strong portfolio. Her success is due to a number of factors, but one is her ability to make decisions quickly, without letting fear or other emotions interfere. In an interview I conducted with her, she related the following story to illustrate how successful people take action based on cool-headed discernment of cash flow potential:

At one point when she was ready to add another property to her portfolio, Laure contacted her trusted realtor. The realtor sent her five listings, and Laure booked a showing for one of them. She stopped at a coffee shop on the way to see the property and did calculations on a napkin to see potential cash flow.

Based on the location and description of the triplex in question, she determined that it not only had existing cash flow potential, but it was also possible to legally add a fourth unit, increasing the return on her investment even more. She went to the showing, liked what she saw, and formulated an offer that represented a good deal to her. Then she immediately wrote her realtor a check. She had gone into the deal already clear that it matched her investment goals, took action, and now the property is performing well for her.

While women are sometimes accused of allowing their emotions to overly influence their buying decisions, this can work to our advantage when the emotion that fuels us is *passion*. When we remain aware of the passionate 'why' behind our goals as real estate investors, we have an invaluable way to discern whether or not a given opportunity can help us attain them. This ability to keep our eyes on the prize allows us to focus our energy on those investment opportunities with the most potential to satisfy us, simplifying both our businesses and our lives.

Doing Due Diligence is Pivotal

Once I made the decision to invest, I went around looking for partners. Initial presentations met with a number of "no"s so I went with people who knew me, my friends, and other property investors. When I showed them the numbers and explained my exit strategies, a number of them were convinced enough to partner with me.

I obtained a referral for a mortgage broker from my real estate agent. Trusting the recommendation proved to be a liability and I failed to conduct sufficient due diligence. The mortgage broker was shady and was later found to be involved in fraudulent practices. The long and short of it all was that I managed to back out of the transaction but was short of a mortgage, and I had partners waiting impatiently. With another recommendation in hand, I did my homework to make sure the second mortgage broker was above board. Thankfully, the transaction was free of fuss and hassle, and met all legalities and ethics. It was a stressful process in the beginning but, with grace, everything turned out alright in the end.

I stuck it out with the purchase because it's in a high-demand, high-growth area. My research into past trends and current demographic changes suggests that demand for housing in this area will stay robust for years to come. I live close to my investment, I'm able to keep an eye out on any market changes. Acclaimed author and real estate investment coach Patrick McKernan illustrates these principles beautifully in an article entitled *7 Steps to Better Investing* in the online version of *Canadian Real Estate Magazine*. His approach centres on the formulation of authentic goals that reflect what you're passionate about creating in your life. These goals will help you keep your eyes on the prize that matters to you, not to someone else. He offers the following observation drawn from his experiences coaching people to success in real estate investment:

The biggest difference between successful and unsuccessful real estate investors comes down to their plan and the authenticity behind it. In other words, why do they want to achieve their real estate goals, and do they firmly believe in the 'why' behind the plan?

Women's talent for keeping our eyes on the big picture gives us an advantage in the vital process of goal-setting. Taking the time to envision the life you want to create and articulate how real estate investing will help you get there can go a long way towards ensuring success.

Of course, change is the only constant in life, and you should always revisit your goals periodically to be sure they still reflect your vision. Precisely because there are so many details to keep track of in real estate investing, you will save yourself boatloads of time and energy by setting aside time to develop goals that inspire you.

Reaching Your Why

Acclaimed Canadian real-estate investor and coach Julie Broad addresses this point very nicely in a blog on her website, www.revnyou.com. On the subject of goals, she writes:

I have learned that it's good to have an idea of where you're going, but always look at the bigger picture of WHY you're doing what you're doing. For us, as real estate investors, we weren't looking to create an empire. We wanted to create freedom and options. Once we reached that, we slowed our pace of acquisition down dramatically.

We hadn't reached a magical number [of properties] – we had reached our why.

Like many coaches, Julie advocates a 'buy and hold' strategy that's designed to create wealth over the long term, not overnight. She repeatedly points out that, while everyone wants to make it big, money by itself is a terrible motivator. Most people aren't motivated enough by it to push through when the going gets tough, if their only goal is to get rich, and that's where a passionate 'why' is so important.

For his part, Philip McKernan believes that people are only truly passionate about three things: family, spirituality, and contribution. These happen to be areas where women already tend to place emphasis in their lives, which can work to our advantage in the goal-setting process. Like Julie's 'freedom and options,' the best investment goals reflect your deepest aspirations for your life, reminding you of why facing the challenges of becoming a real estate investor is worthwhile to you.

These passion-fueled goals will help you keep your eyes on the prize as you face the many choices involved with assembling an investment team and buying properties. In real estate, you need discernment at every step of the process, from assessing potential partners and tenants to catching loopholes buried in the legalese surrounding mortgages and rental agreements. You need to engage in every interaction and every step of each process with as much awareness as possible, so you can catch pesky details that might crop up and cause trouble later.

In a blog article on how to avoid some of the most common real estate investment mistakes, Julie Broad puts it this way:

Ever seen the movie UP? The cartoon dogs in the movie are on a very serious mission. They are focused and moving quickly towards their goal … until they spot a squirrel!

Suddenly all attention is directed to the squirrel and they are no longer worried about their plan.

This is what seems to happen to a lot of investors. They either don't have an investment plan to follow so they are always looking for squirrels, or they allow themselves to get easily distracted from that plan when a new squirrel appears.

Sticking to a well thought out plan, based on the fundamentals of real estate investment (buying for cash flow in areas with good economic fundamentals), instead of chasing the latest deal destination will help you make more money, put in less effort and minimize the risks in your investments dramatically.

Flow Matters

Putting a solid plan in place is step one, but patience and persistence are required to implement it, and these are two qualities that many women possess in abundance. However, I want to address here the importance of balancing persistence with *going with the flow*. While a certain amount of frustration is normal with such a complex endeavour as real estate investment, it's also important to recognize the signs that perhaps a particular property or partnership just isn't meant to be. Julie Broad has a 'three strikes and you're out' policy that she swears by; she'll consider overlooking one or two minor problems in a property, but as soon as a third one crops up she backs out. This is her way of discerning the right action when she finds herself faced with the choice of either pushing ahead or letting go.

I want to take a moment here to relate an old Chinese parable I love, which illustrates this point in a profound way. From it, we learn that refraining from judgment about our life situations can prevent us from jumping to unfounded conclusions regarding the twists and turns of fate. You may wish to photocopy this story and keep it near at hand as you begin your journey with real estate investment.

The Old Farmer: Fortune, or Misfortune?

Once upon a time, there was an old farmer who had worked his crops for many years. One day his only horse ran away. Upon hearing the news, his neighbors came to visit. "Such bad luck," they said sympathetically. "Maybe," the farmer replied. The next morning the horse returned, bringing with it three other wild horses. "How wonderful," the neighbors exclaimed. "Maybe," replied the old man. The following day, his son tried to ride one of the untamed horses, was thrown, and broke his leg. The neighbors again came to offer their sympathy on his misfortune. "Maybe," answered the farmer. The following day, military officials came to the village to draft young men into the army. Seeing that the son's leg was broken, they passed him by. The neighbors congratulated the farmer on how well things had turned out. "Maybe," said the farmer.

Or, as William Shakespeare so aptly put it, "There is nothing either good or bad, but thinking makes it so." The first rule that Patrick McKernan lists in his article on success in real estate investing is to be *realistic* about where you are financially and emotionally before getting started, so you can create goals that are achievable and meaningful to you. On the other hand, however, many other investment coaches exhort beginning investors to overcome 'analysis paralysis,' and *just act.* Clearly, it is balance that is called for here, and discernment will lead you there.

With passion-based goals, a solid plan and network, and the right guidance, a woman's ability to keep her eyes on the prize will take her far on the road to success with real estate investment. Ralph Waldo Emerson puts it so beautifully when he says:

Dare to live the life you have dreamed for yourself. Go forward and make your dreams come true.

Raymond and I hope this book will help you do just that!

This is a particularly vital skill to have at every step of the real estate investment process, from networking to buying properties, and women tend to do it very well.

Our ability as women to combine being detail-oriented with discernment based on the big picture gives us a definite advantage in the world of real estate investment.

Chapter 3
Cutting Through the Crap

There is no scientific answer for success. You can't define it. You've
simply got to live it and do it.
– Anita Roddick, founder of The Body Shop

I love this quote from highly-successful female entrepreneur
Anita Roddick, because it shows that, while there is value in
learning from experts and books, ultimately success comes from
the ability to take action.

The ability to take successful action, in turn, is tied to what I call
cutting through the crap. While the discernment I spoke of in
the previous chapter is about noticing details and keeping your
awareness on your goals at all times, cutting through the crap
means not being afraid to confront yourself and others when the
situation demands it. This is another skill area in which women
often excel, because the roles we play in life tend to foster in us
an understanding of the fact that, the sooner you confront an
issue, the less likely it is to blow up in your face.

Law of Confront

I've heard this principle referred to as the Law of Confront, which states that your ability to confront issues as they arise determines the degree of simplicity you will experience in your life. For example, a $25 parking ticket is a pain, but if you don't pay it off promptly it will accrue interest over time, until eventually your car could be impounded and you could face hundreds of dollars in fines.

The higher the stakes in a given situation, the more relevant this principle becomes, and real estate is a high-stakes endeavour. For this reason, it's even more important to be real with yourself and others involved when your realize something's off. Though they may not say it out loud, many people will be grateful to you for voicing what they perhaps didn't want to admit to themselves.

Why a Naysayer Matters

Julie Broad speaks eloquently to this point. She says that the role she considers most vital to fill on your real estate investment team is that of the Naysayer. This is someone knowledgeable about real estate, but unrelated to you and divested of any interest in how your deals go. Their one and only job is to alert you to red flags you may be missing due to what might be called the Law of Self-Justification, which acts as a sort of counter-principle to the Law of Confront. Julie puts it this way:

The bigger the investment of time, money and energy into something you've voluntarily chosen to pursue, the more attractive that something becomes to you. In other words, the more effort you put into finding and negotiating a deal, securing the funding, or presenting to that potential investor, the less likely you are to process future information pertaining to that person/opportunity accurately.

Many of us already have examples from our personal lives of the valuable role that a Naysayer has played at one point or another. Have you ever changed your mind about a major decision as a result of reflection offered by such a person, and later been very glad you did? You don't want to buy the wrong property any more than you want to take the wrong job or, heaven forbid, marry the wrong man. For this reason, a good Naysayer is well worth her weight in gold. While a close friend or relative may have filled this role for you in the past, I want to emphasize that, when it comes to your investment goals, such people are often prone to letting fear colour their advice. That's why it's so important to fill the role of Naysayer for your business with someone who can remain neutral.

Due to the financial implications of your real estate investment decisions, it is important to fill the role of Naysayer on your team with someone who is not a close friend or relative. Julie Broad says that she and her husband have almost always filled the role of Naysayer with a paid mentor or coach, but it can be filled by anyone in your network whom you feel you can trust. She refers to a book entitled <u>*Mistakes Were Made, But Not By Me*</u>, whose authors, Carol Travis and Elliot Aronson, state the importance of including such a person on your team:

"We need a few trusted naysayers in our lives. Critics who are willing to puncture our protective bubble of self-justification and yank us back to reality if we veer too far off."

I want to be sure you realize that the role of a Naysayer is not simply to be critical. That's where trust comes in. In our roles as wives, daughters, sisters, mothers, and friends, many women learn that confronting ourselves and others is made much easier when compassion and understanding are brought to the table. We all struggle with confrontation from time to time, so there's no need to make it personal; it's about gently directing your awareness to what you may be avoiding. Have you carefully determined your maximum allowable offer for a given property? Are you letting emotional attachment to one aspect of it, like that fabulous chef's kitchen, get the better of you? Good coaches are highly trained in the art of compassionate confrontation, yet another reason to hire a coach as you set out to implement your real estate investment plan.

Commitment to compassionate confront is only one of many reasons why women excel at cutting through the crap. On a more mundane level, when you're in charge of managing a household, you quickly learn to think on your feet. As a stay-at-home mom, I often didn't have the luxury of reflecting much before making decisions, because I was always busy dealing with little emergencies.

You Are Already Skilled at Cutting Through The Crap

My time management skills improved after my daughter was born. They had to if I ever wanted to get anything done. I had to re-adjust life to meet the demands of this new addition to the family, which were always changing as she got older and entered into a new phase of challenges. I always needed to adjust and balance my time to focus on what was more urgent, and other tasks that were still important, but not so urgent. I honed my ability to stay focused on what matters, out of necessity.

The net result is that I'm much less likely now to waste time on things that are not working than I used to be, and more likely to assess situations accurately the first time around. This is a skill that has served me very well in real estate investment. While women may rightfully complain about the challenges of "Having it all" in this day and age, those same challenges have trained us to hone in on what's true and sharpening this skill for years, so why not put the training life's given you to use in service of your investment goals?

Like someone who learns to swim by being thrown into the water, I learned to manage my time down to the minute when my daughter was born. Throughout her infancy and early childhood, I honed my ability to stay focused on what matters, out of necessity.

Even if you're a professional with no children, working full-time outside the home, you still need to create work-life balance. The skills you develop from these efforts transfer very well to real estate investing for several reasons. As I'm sure you know by now, investing in real estate is a complex, multi-step process in which you must manage many details simultaneously. There are many choices to consider: do you stick to residential properties, or add office, industrial, or retail titles to your portfolio? What locations make the most sense for you to buy in? When you consider that women combine prowess at multi-tasking with a talent for keeping our eyes on our goals and spotting red flags, it's clear that we bring a distinct advantage to the complex real estate investment game.

There's another realm in which women are adept at cutting through the crap that I find very interesting. I don't know about you, but I've observed that, within couples and families, women often act as custodians of familial harmony. We're the ones who call a family meeting when there's something that needs to be aired, and the ones who probe our partners to communicate when something feels off.

Sometimes we even feel as though the whole family might fall apart if we weren't there to play the role of manager / therapist. I'm not saying this is a good or bad thing, or that it isn't artificially imposed on us by society in large part. The point is, we often find ourselves in the role of facilitating a confrontation that others may be avoiding, and this is an invaluable talent in real estate. No one likes to waste time and money and, as I mentioned before, others will secretly thank you for uncovering the truth even if they don't say it out loud.

It's important to remember that, as an investor, you're choosing to buy a product – property – in an effort to generate returns on your investment as well as your time. The people you are buying from, however, are motivated chiefly by the desire to get the best possible price for the goods they're selling – that's capitalism in a nutshell, right? This inevitably creates a tendency on the part of sellers (and their agents) to tell less than the whole truth about their property to one degree or another, and it's up to the buyer to ask the tough questions and do their due diligence before finalizing the purchase.

Even well-intentioned sellers aren't immune to the temptation to omit details that might raise concerns for a potential buyer. When you know how to cut through the crap as an investor, you can save yourself and your business partners loads of time, energy, and money spent pursuing properties that turn out to be more trouble than they're worth.

It is essential to find the right home inspector. The Ontario government will now regulate the home inspection industry with a licensing requirement that helps to protect home buyers. This will be helpful in minimizing bad risks.

Select a home inspector that is highly recognized in the industry, or you may end up with a leaky roof or bad plumbing or electric circuitry after you have signed the agreement, which may land you with big repair bills.

When you demonstrate your commitment to making decisions based on the truth, the whole truth, and nothing but the truth, you become very attractive to investment partners who want a trustworthy team member with whom to share their wealth and knowledge. You're also more likely to cross paths with property managers, lawyers, accountants, bankers, realtors, and tenants who share similar values.

If you aim to always tell the truth to yourself and others, you attract people committed to doing the same, and this will go a very long way to making your journey with real estate investment less complicated and more enjoyable. After all, your real estate investment business should make you leap out of bed in the morning – if it doesn't, something's wrong!

If, like many beginning investors, you decide to include residential properties in your portfolio, your skills in cutting through the crap will be fired in the kiln of your interactions with tenants and property managers. The importance of precaution in contracting such people cannot be underestimated. The quality of your tenants determines not only the consistency of the rental income that a property produces, but the wear and tear it sustains, as well as the community's perception of you and the property itself.

While the pool of applicants you attract will depend a great deal on the desirability of the neighborhood the property is located in, even in the best areas you need to keep an eye out for anything fishy on the rental application. Of course good people don't always look that way on paper, and this is why references are so important. It's incumbent upon you to ask the questions that need to be asked of both potential tenants and their references, in order to get a clear picture of a prospective lessee's suitability for your needs.

By the time you have more than a small handful of properties in your portfolio, you'll likely be ready to add a property manager to your team who can take care of maintenance, leasing, or both. He or she acts as a liaison between you and your tenants, taking much of the day-to-day responsibility for managing your properties off your shoulders so you can be free to grow your business, or simply enjoy more leisure time. Clearly, you need this person to be extremely trustworthy, and someone with a good reputation is worth paying a premium for. When you know how to cut through the crap, you stand a better chance of hiring a property manager who will make your life easier, not harder!

When to Say Yes

As we conclude this chapter, let's review how we determine what to say 'yes' to as investors. As you can probably guess by now, the answer lies in whether or not saying 'yes' will move us closer to the goals that motivated us to begin investing in real estate in the first place. Remember, 'making money' doesn't count: your choices need to be framed in light of the deeper reasons behind why you got into real estate.

A property may offer a high return on investment, but is it the right fit for you if it's going to require many hours of your time to turn a profit, and your goal is to balance earning income with increasing leisure time? When you put in the work to get super-clear on your goals, you won't be afraid to take action when you find a property that matches them, or to say no to one that doesn't.

The ability to discern when to take action as an investor comes as you refine your goals and gain experience with what works for you and what doesn't. Then investing can become a game that you genuinely enjoy, and that helps you create the life of your dreams. The only way to get better is to keep playing, even if you lose some of the time because, as with any game, 'practice makes perfect.'

Chapter 4
Networking Through Nurturing Relationships

I've learned that people will forget what you said, people will forget what you did, but people will never forget how you made them feel.
– Maya Angelou

In the discussions that Raymond and I have had about networking over the course of our coaching relationship, I've realized the power of what Maya Angelou speaks to in the quote above. I've learned that making a special effort to listen to and remember details about the people I meet has more power to strengthen my network than almost anything else. Because you know what? When you make someone feel seen, heard, and valued, they will remember you when they're sharing contacts with other people in their networks, and this has the potential to increase the payoff from the time you spend networking exponentially.

If you were a talkative child, you may have heard the following adage from the adults around you more than once: "God gave us two ears and one mouth, so we should listen at least twice as much as we talk." The more time I've spent networking, the more respect I've developed for this homespun wisdom. The ability that women have to listen deeply helps us come across as not only caring but intelligent, and this is never a bad thing when your goal is to attract quality investment partners. In an entertaining piece on her website entitled *An Introvert's Guide to Real Estate Investing Success*, Julie Broad says,

It's a funny thing that happens when you listen more than you speak – the person you are speaking with thinks you're smart, probably because you're listening to them!

So you see, women's ability to listen deeply to potential partners can go a long way towards strengthening those ties, so they'll be there when you need them.

Whether we are moms, teachers, artists, or businesswomen, we understand that the success of both our personal and professional relationships depends on striking an ideal balance between listening and speaking. If we were fortunate, our role models showed us the power of small gestures of caring to strengthen both family and community. Our mothers encouraged us to write thank-you cards for gifts received at birthdays and holidays, help out elderly neighbours, and make a special effort to befriend the new girl at school. These consistent lessons in the power of caring, compassion, and connection gave us a strong foundation on which to build fulfilling lives, whether we play the role of homemaker, executive, or anything else. Central to this is the understanding that all people have a deep need to be seen, heard and valued for who they truly are, and this is no less true of realtors and bankers than it is of anyone else.

Success = Strength of Your Network

I want to take a moment here to highlight something very important about real estate investing: *perhaps more than with any other endeavour, the strength of your network will determine your success*. It doesn't matter whether you plan to employ a buy-and-hold strategy, or feel confident undertaking riskier ventures like renovating and flipping houses, you need the right people on your team to bring your dreams to fruition. There are few, if any, recognized experts in REI who invest on their own, much less advocate this strategy for others. The simple truth is that investing in property is a complex and expensive undertaking, and it is well worth sharing profits with business partners in exchange for their contributions of time, expertise, or funds.

My partners in my property investment saw what the earlier naysayers, who turned down my plan, didn't. The target property, a house, was a diamond in the rough. It had good bones but it needed a facelift and a lot of elbow grease. I was blessed in finding those partners who shared my vision because teamwork gets you much further than attempting to do it alone. Specifically, my partners came in in full force when I faced difficulties with the fraudulent mortgage broker, and they directed me to the right professional in a timely manner. Otherwise, the property would have been sold to another buyer who was waiting on the sidelines.

Once we received the keys to the house, we got to work. We took away the tired burgundy walls that served only to darken the property and freshened up the house with a warm, neutral colour. We chose a fresh white for the baseboards and removed the graffiti-laden doors with new ones with contemporary designs.

Any fan of HGTV knows that bathroom remodeling (likewise for kitchens) get you the biggest bang for the buck. The previous owner, who was clearly into do-it-yourself, tried to renovate but failed in our books. He tiled the bathroom but didn't finish his attempts to tile the walls and inexplicably, left a finger-shaped smear of grout on the tiles! My mother had the bathroom torn down and remodeled with modern vanities, faucets, toilets and bathtub. Right now, the property is rented out to tenants, whom we screened carefully. The rent more than pays the monthly mortgage, and our current plan is to hold onto the property for further appreciation.

I needed to stage the place to attract rental clients, but I didn't want to spend money on hiring a professional stager. I was further reluctant to pay retail prices for furniture that had a short-lived purpose. Instead, I took a stroll around the neighbourhood and found some great pieces left out on the sidewalk for the garbage man. My first find was a solid wooden kitchen table with matching chairs. My next find was a couch with very nice lines. It need a little upgrade so I had it steam-cleaned and gave it a makeover by hiding the flaws under a neutral colored couch cover and decorative pillows. With my third find, a coffee table, my staging requirements were fully met. Buffed and polished with wood oil, the coffee table looked as good as new.

Finding the right tenants can be tricky. We wanted only those people who would take care of the house as if it was their own, and I used a timeless method, which has never failed me. For every tenant I meet, I check out the condition of their car, if they have one. If the car is shabby and filled with rusty dents, that is a no-no in my books. If their car is well maintained and kept clean, then they become serious contenders for tenancy. This is a simple device to separate the wheat from the chaff, so to speak. I believe in this saying, "how you do anything is how you do everything."

If the prospective tenants couldn't keep their car tidy, there is no likelihood they will do the same for my property!

Partnership as a Key to Success

On her website at RevNYou.com, Julie Broad posts an article entitled '5 Tips for Successful Real Estate Partnerships' in which she shares the following thoughts on her journey of building wealth with real estate:

As I reflect back on the things that my husband and I did in the last eight years to become millionaires – I think that **finding good properties in areas with promising economic futures, and buying them with good partners was the key to our success.**

She expands on this key point elsewhere:

The best deals usually come from within your network. Realtors or mortgage brokers with their ear to the ground are a great source of deals. You have to get plugged in to the people who can find you great deals.

If you are someone who doesn't have money to buy real estate - networking is critical. We've been able to build a nice sized portfolio not because we did no money down deals or because we had a lot of money but because we found a few partners with money to invest with us. They didn't have time or knowledge … we took the time to build the knowledge and became their partners.

These words from a highly successful woman real estate investor highlight just how crucial networking is to success. A good network can supply you with deals whether you have cash at the ready or not, and if you don't have funds of your own available, it can help you connect with good investment partners. This is why a good network is crucial to success.

Don't Shortchange the Practice

You know that building your web of contacts is important, but developing the skill to leverage your network effectively takes practice. Fortunately, as I touched on at the beginning of this chapter, your life as a woman has likely already set you up to succeed. I know that, when I became a mother, the value I placed on my social support network skyrocketed, because raising children is really hard to do on your own, even with a highly supportive partner. Children are like little benevolent dictators, enormously demanding both financially and time-wise. So from the beginning as a parent, there's a strong incentive to create and maintain an informal network of friends and neighbours who support you, and whom you support in return. While it's not always obvious these days that it takes a village to raise a child, any parent will tell you that the task is much easier with a strong social network in place.

When you're just starting out, there's no reason you can't begin to mention your goals as a real estate investor to everyone you encounter in your daily life, right from the beginning. You never know what unexpected connections your hairdresser might have that could be useful to you, and the same goes for the parents of your children's friends if you have kids. The goals of your networking will change over time, as your focus naturally evolves from learning the ropes to expanding your portfolio. When you treat every connection as valuable, you may be surprised at which ones come in handy at every stage of the journey.

When you decide to invest in real estate, the first leg of your journey consists of becoming comfortable with core skills such as setting up your business, market research, mortgages and titling, and how different types of real estate respond to different economic conditions. This is important because, as I've learned in my experience as a real estate investor and in my work with Raymond, it's true that success is all about winning your Inner Game. That is, *the leverage you get out of networking is proportional to the confidence you feel in your passion, knowledge, and abilities as an investor.*

If you don't come across as confident, people won't be inspired to align their interests with yours, or to pass your name on to their own networks. Benjamin Franklin said that "an investment in knowledge always pays the best interest," and I believe the payoff from such an investment is much greater than simply being better informed. Knowledge will help you believe in yourself, and project the confidence to attract collaborators who can help you reach your goals.

All this aside, however, building your knowledge base is only one aspect of building confidence. It doesn't matter how many books you read or seminars you attend; the key to projecting confidence is a *willingness* to act. You can impress people with your exhaustive knowledge of current market conditions or investment strategies, but if you don't project a clear intention to act on your knowledge, you will lose people's interest. Sometimes it's just a matter of willpower, and sometimes you need to mentally map out your worst fears to convince yourself that you can overcome them. In any case, the intention to act, combined with confidence inspired by clear goals, is a recipe for success with real estate investment and many other things as well.

Why Women Come Ahead

There are several reasons why women can come out ahead in the networking game, particularly those who have some experience as professionals.

As you prepare to enter the world of real estate investment, there are two positive outgrowths from this: first, you may already be accustomed to pushing yourself to excel, and second, real estate is an entrepreneurial industry in which the playing field for women is relatively level, so your efforts to shine will be well-received. I believe that the growing number of women who have had success with real estate attests to this.

As we touched on earlier, the caring and helpful mindset that women are socialized to have helps us remember important details about the people we meet, and look for ways to collaborate for mutual benefit. Our ability to ask insightful questions and listen deeply to the answers ensures that the people we speak to feel seen, heard, and valued, so they will be more likely to remember us. Finally, these traits combine to make us excellent judges of character, an invaluable asset when screening potential tenants or assembling the team you need to help with each aspect of investing.

Laure Ampilhac, whom I interviewed for this book, has a helpful perspective on the way you can use these skills to build your team. In our conversations, she told me about how she is working to build relationships with her tenants and to bring a sense of community to a property she recently purchased. She trusted her intuition during the screening process, found great tenants as a result, and now one of her tenants does the showings for her and has helped bring in another great tenant. As anyone who invests in residential property will tell you, there is nothing more crucial to your cash flow than maintaining uninterrupted occupancy, so this significantly improves the profitability of Laure's business. In the same way that people with money tend to know other people with money, good tenants tend to have connections to other good tenants, helping you to maintain continuous occupancy in the residential properties you own.

Laure's ability to delegate the task of finding tenants to her existing tenant is only one example of how the time and effort that she puts into her relationships ends up making her life easier down the road. She also appointed a trusted tenant as property manager, decreasing the amount of time she personally needs to spend maintaining the property. She attributes her ability to attract and keep great tenants to her policy of responding immediately any time one of them needs something. If she did not take the time to get to know her tenants and build relationships with them, she would most likely experience more stress as a landlord.

Better, Deeper Relationships

It's clear that time devoted to relationship-building is time well spent in real estate investing, and women excel at the kind of networking that involves building deep relationships over time.

We are better listeners, and we build our network of relationships by showing others that we genuinely care. Already skilled in the art of relationship, all we need to do is to cast our net wider to power up our networking. You can think of it as tending a garden, planting seeds all around and giving them the care and attention they need to some day blossom into mighty trees. We know how to make people feel valued, inspiring them to value us as well, and connect us with others in their networks.

I'd like to say a few words here about the importance of giving back. I've emphasized repeatedly that success in REI is not something that most people can achieve alone. As you pursue your dreams, you will rely on support from people both known and unknown at every stage of the process. I believe that looking for opportunities to help others improve their lives is a sure-fire way to expand your own success. I fully believe this to be true. Remember at each stage of your journey that you stand on the shoulders of others, and in recognition of our interconnection, be available to offer support and help others who are in need.

With knowledge, confidence, and the commitment to act, women can walk into networking events poised to form fruitful connections that last. Once you've perfected your inner game, chances are good that you will create high-leverage connections in a fairly short period of time, and this is your ticket to finding the deals that will generate solid cash flow. Julie Broad sums it up nicely in one of her posts:

The single greatest factor in our success in the four years since I left my job has been the fact that we have hired great coaches to help us at each stage as we grew, we invested in our own personal growth, and we traveled the country to meet the best people to know. We invested a lot of time and money to escalate, grow and improve the people we were surrounding ourselves with.

From this statement, it's clear that an investment in yourself can yield excellent returns for your real estate business, provided it's founded on authentic goals that motivate you to stay committed. The recipe for success is easy to concoct when the ingredients have ripened, and as a woman, you may already have a bounty ready to pick.

Chapter 5
Follow Up to Follow Through

Have a bias toward action – let's see something happen now. You can break that big plan into small steps and take the first step right away.
– Indira Gandhi

These words from one of history's most influential female heads of state make it clear that, while preparation is important, the way to reach your goals is to have a 'bias towards action.' In the previous chapter, we explored how the care and intuitive awareness that women bring to networking allow us to form long-term connections founded on trust and mutual benefit. When we make a strong commitment to following up and following through with those connections, we gain the ability to quickly bring our goals within sight.

Because women naturally treasure connections with others, we are willing to put in the time and effort required to make our connections bear fruit. We remember small details that were mentioned in conversation, which help us to form a complete picture of each contact in our network. We can then use this information to make each one feel seen, heard and valued when we follow up with them. We know that making this a priority does a great deal to ensure that the people we meet remember us when they are looking for investment partners, or sharing contacts with other connections in their networks.

The hallmark of successful networking is when your contacts begin connecting you with other people they know because they feel confident it will lead to positive experiences for all involved. When you demonstrate your commitment to integrity, listening, and respect in all your interactions, you greatly increase the likelihood that your contacts will activate their own networks on your behalf.

The Other Elements of Success

I want to point out here that keeping your network energized and active is only one aspect of following up and following through. Another is dedicating time, money and energy to all of the tasks required to grow your business. Laure Ampilhac often reminds her coaching clients that, while knowledge comes from learning, confidence comes mostly from experience. This means that the more willing you are to act on good deals when you find them, the more confident you'll become activating your network to take advantage of them. When your commitment to due diligence is high and your goals are clear, you will be in a position to add cash flowing properties to your portfolio fairly quickly. Then, even if one or two properties underperform or become problematic, you'll have the confidence to learn from these experiences, so they add to your credibility instead of deflating it.

On the subject of credibility, it is important to understand that, while you must establish it to attract good investing partners, you don't need an MBA or an impressive portfolio to be credible. Taking the time to practice your pitch as a real estate investor and do the research to back up your statements can go a long way. You immediately establish credibility when you can reference specific statistics about your investment area, and speak intelligently and in depth about market projections. If you combine this with a friendly demeanour, present your existing experience in the best possible light, and leverage any 'credibility by association' with respected coaches and mentors, you will be well positioned to add high-quality people to your pool of potential partners.

Once you've clarified the type and number of properties you wish to add to your portfolio, you can begin shopping around for the ones that represent the best return on your investments of money and time. It's important to remember that you may need to look at dozens of properties before you find one that matches your goals closely enough to be a really good deal for you. Then you will need to coordinate the purchase with your realtor, mortgage broker, and other members of your team to ensure that all the details are taken care of. You have to be prepared to do a fair bit of running around every time you're working to close a deal. You could say that real estate investing requires you to perfect the art of the hustle.

In an article on RevNYou.com entitled *10 Reasons Real Estate Investors Underperform*, Dave Peniuk lists this as point #8. In this context, hustling simply means the ability to juggle all the tasks involved with making deals in real estate, to keep the whole thing moving forward. These include lining up partners, completing financial and legal paperwork, communicating with members of your team, getting inspections and appraisals done, etc. This is where women's natural talent for multi-tasking, thinking on our feet, and being persistent can combine to serve us very well.

As both Dave and Julie often say in their writings on RevNYou.com, when you make offers that are conditional on inspection, financing, or both, you give yourself time (usually 5 business days) to take care of due diligence and back out if you choose to without penalty. This is why it is so important to take action; even if you do decide to back out of a particular deal, you still will have gained valuable experience that adds to your confidence and credibility. There's nothing wrong with making offers, so just do it!

No Substitute for Just Doing It

I found a great real-world example of this in the story of a young man named Gene, as told to Dr. Steve Sjuggerud at www.investmentu.com. Gene started investing in real estate in his early twenties, while he was still enrolled in a master's degree program at the University of Florida in Gainesville. He managed to turn a nice profit just by following his instincts; in fact he was so successful that he never even looked for a job in his field after graduating, devoting himself full-time to becoming the best real estate investor he could be.

Figuring that the success he'd had might have just been beginner's luck, he enrolled in every real estate investing course he could find, and tried every strategy they advocated for turning profits fast. Still, he found that nothing was profitable for him as the strategy that he was intuitively drawn to as a student.

What was that strategy? Dr. Sjuggerud relates it as follows:

Here's one of Gene's central real estate secrets: He says he buys middle-to-lower class properties on the fringe of good neighborhoods. He only buys at what he considers to be a 20% discount or more to the market value of the property. And he only buys when he can NET 8%+ a year in rent. That's it. After trying all the hype, this is what works for him.

Gene makes sure that the rents he'll get immediately will give him that 8% or more profit margin per year, but he sets himself up to make much greater future profits by purchasing lower-value properties that may one day be engulfed by adjacent, more prosperous neighborhoods. By following through on the strategy that made intuitive sense to him, he discovered a way to reliably exceed his projected profits as a professional real estate investor, year after year.

Gene may be a man, but his success is due in no small measure to a trait that is more often associated with women: listening to intuition. It's true that most of us will not experience his degree of clarity regarding our ideal investment strategy without getting a solid education first. But have you ever experienced a sense of knowing that went against your logical mind, and been glad when you listened to it? While the article does not go into detail regarding how Gene developed his strategy, it seems that it is not something that he sat down and thought out. Rather, he employed it because, based on what he observed on the ground and on some rudimentary knowledge of investing, it made intuitive sense to him. From his story, we learn that the best investment strategies often involve striking the perfect balance between hands-on market research and going with your gut.

The Major Ps

While the article does not explicitly speak to this, I believe that Gene also possesses another crucial trait that is often more closely associated with women: *patience*. While all women have plenty of practice with patience, this is another area where mothers deserve gold medals. It is amazing how strong the wills of young children can be. As mothers, we learn that sometimes the most effective tactic is to simply stop engaging with the unreasonable child and wait patiently while the tantrum runs its course. While we wait, we may turn our attention to taking care of some small task, or reflect on how to help the child process their feelings when the storm has passed. These are skills that can serve us very well in real estate investing, as we multi-task to maintain momentum for several deals at once, or wait for reluctant partners to come around.

Like so many things in life, however, patience must be balanced with another quality that complements it: persistence. As an investor, I have abundant personal experience with the importance of persistence in getting deals done. For example, I once saw a property, did some research and calculations, and decided I wanted to purchase it. I lined up a partner, but they backed out before I could make an offer.

Not wanting to miss out on this deal, I called another investor who wasn't interested. Undeterred, I called up a real estate agent who I knew wanted to buy her first investment. She agreed that the investment looked great, but said it would only work for her if I became her client, yet I'm already signed with an agent, so that prospect wasn't attractive to me. I kept looking and, as mentioned in the earlier chapters, I found the right combination of partners.

While some real estate investment educators recommend exploring joint venture investments with friends and family to get started, in my own experience I've found that this isn't always the best option. I once made a well-supported case for both my father and my sister to invest with me, but was met with resistance because they lack an investor's mindset and therefore see any involvement with real estate as risky.

I quickly learned that by attending seminars about real estate investing provided me with access to like-minded people who understand the mechanics behind investing. Meeting people who share similar goals and interests is a great way to share experiences as to what worked for you, and what didn't work, and there are always opportunities to learn something new and grow from these meetings.

Persistence is crucial for all aspects of real estate investment, but especially for finding investment partners, as these examples from my own life illustrate. When my family members were reluctant to partner with me, I turned instead to a mortgage broker who had experience with raising private money for investments, and have learned a lot from this relationship. Because each of us will have a unique situation, it's very important not to get discouraged when a strategy that others claim has worked for them doesn't work for you. This is why you need powerful, inspiring goals to keep your motivation high when things get bumpy, so you can do what it takes to bring success within reach.

The most effective goals inspire action, but they are also worth waiting for. While women may not always be immune to the desire for instant gratification, the experiences of our lives may inoculate us against the tendency to underestimate the effort required to succeed.

Whether we have built a career outside the home or not, if we are mothers, we will have had abundant experience with both patience and persistence. In our efforts to prepare our children for the realities of the adult world, we may make a special effort to help them develop the capacity for delayed gratification. We know that, if we resist the urge to spoil them and ask them instead to buy things they want with their hard-earned allowance money, they will learn the value of saving and spending wisely. If they show interest in sports or music, we encourage them to practice every day so they will be ready for the big game or performance. As women, we often find ourselves in the role of modeling both patience and perseverance, and encouraging the development of these qualities in our family members.

With patience, persistence, and trust in your intuition, you will be ready to follow up and follow through to maximize your success as a real estate investor. You will have what it takes to act on your vision and create the life you want for yourself and your loved ones.

Chapter 6
A Keen Eye for a Deal

Dare to live the life you have dreamed for yourself. Go forward and make your dreams come true.
— Ralph Waldo Emerson

So far, we have discussed five ways in which women's natural talents and abilities set us up for success with real estate investing. In this chapter, we are going to bring it all together to show you how they all combine to make women Masters of the Deal. In real estate as with any other market, your profit margin is largely determined by your ability to find quality products and pay below market value for them. This is the essence of a truly good deal.

If you've spent any time at all around people who invest in real estate or have done any reading on the subject, you know that success is all about finding and purchasing properties that offer exceptional value for the price. You always want to look for undervalued properties and pursue them before they even get listed if possible, which is easy to do once you know the right people. Also, as a savvy investor, you always want to pay wholesale prices, not retail. If you have a membership with a wholesale grocery chain or have ever bought cut flowers from a wholesaler, you know how much money this can save you! Any woman who has ever pulled off a beautiful wedding or other special event on a tight budget knows the immense satisfaction of doing what it takes to find the best deals, thereby creating value above and beyond what might seem possible. If such moments are among your most treasured memories, then you will no doubt find much to enjoy in the process of growing your real estate portfolio.

Your Best Deal is Created, Not Found

While market research - including legwork on the ground - is always a prerequisite for finding great deals, Julie Broad points out that the best deals often aren't found, they are created. She speaks about different ways to create value in properties in many of her writings, from adding a legal suite to negotiating terms that help you make the property more profitable, such as permission to show the property immediately to potential tenants. When you know what terms are that represent a good deal to you, and you know the problem the seller is looking to solve, you're well on your way to creating an excellent deal.

In a video on her blog, Julie shares an example of how she found one of the best properties in her portfolio by working to uncover the seller's perspective so she could solve their biggest problem for them. This particular property was an estate sale of a home that had been occupied for thirty years by an elderly gentleman who had no children. His next of kin were his two sisters who were also getting on in years, and who lived several hours away by car and ferry. When Julie looked at this house filled with decades worth of accumulated stuff, she realized that these two older ladies would probably find dealing with it overwhelming. This gave her the idea to offer to take care of whatever the sisters didn't want in the house, so they could focus on the things that were important to them and on closing the sale so they could return home. Not only did they accept her very low offer, but also she posted photos of the home's contents and listed them as free on an online site, saving herself $10,000 in disposal costs. She eventually added a legal suite to the home, increasing its value to her even more.

Another great real-life example comes from Laure Ampilhac. Like Julie Broad and every other investor who finds success with real estate, she is committed to taking action when she finds a property that meets her investment objectives. Here is the story she emailed to me in response to my request to learn more about how she got started in real estate investing.

***

Here is the story of how I got the Real Estate Investing bug. You will see I am not someone who spends time thinking of excuses why not to buy a property. This will also illustrate the knowledge and education I have gone through to prepare myself for the next stage in my Real Estate Career. It is a fascinating story that I know you will enjoy.

In 2009, I owned a semi-detached brick house in Roncesvalles, an exclusive neighbourhood bordering Toronto's largest park. I had bought the property with my life partner when we both had good jobs, then I bought him out with help from family when we split up. I was living in the house and renting out three rooms to help with the $2500/month mortgage – that was a lot of people to share my kitchen with! In January of that year, I was introduced to real estate investing for the first time. The three-day workshop presented by Robert Kiyosaki's Educational Company, author of the "Rich Dad Poor Dad" best seller, opened my eyes. In that workshop I learned techniques for finding and negotiating real estate deals, and was empowered to make offers with confidence. I also realized that I had home equity sitting in my lovely blue house.

So in April 2009, I took the leap! It was just after the little bubble in real estate and the middle of the economic slowdown in Toronto. I had become a Senior Business Development and Account Manager of an IT data storage company for the territory of Eastern Canada, and was doing relatively well. I decided to sell my property, use the home equity to buy more real estate and start my career as an investor. The market *was hot and I sold my house in 6 days. It was an incredible ride. I was able to generate $150,000 and use this money to further my personal and professional development, knowing that the best investment I could make at that time was in myself.*

What I forgot to mention is that I quit my comfortable job in June 2009 when the lawyer handed me the cheque the day of closing on my house. So I was searching, analyzing, putting in offers, doing due diligence day after day, month after month. As a self-employed person, it became more challenging to get financing. On top of everything, I took an 8-month sabbatical in France. The months passed by and, in the fall of 2010, I woke up with $30,000 left in my bank account. Just enough for a 10% down payment on a $300,000 house!

I told my Realtor that I needed to find a $300,000 triplex in Toronto so I could collect rent without sharing my own space with my tenants. He was doubtful that such a property could be found but, in two weeks, with my tricks learned from another realtor and in the class, I located a $349,000 distressed 2-storey duplex with an in-law suite on Davenport Road that needed TLC. We sent an offer for $300,000 in a snowstorm that was accepted by the motivated seller at $306,000. A steal for Toronto!

As taught in the courses, I used the special offers on my credit cards (1.99%-3.99%) and low interest lines of credit (4.99%) to pay for the $42,000 upgrades of the 3-unit building. I rented the two 1-bedroom *apartments to two young professional couples starting out in life. I refinanced the house in June 2011; thanks to the upgrades and the monthly income of $2,300 generated from the two units, the bank appraised it at $400,000 six months later and gave me a $30,000 second mortgage to pay off my credit cards! Today, I am generating monthly cash flow and am living rent-free in the 3rd unit with sunroom and south-facing backyard.*

Why am I telling you this story? For the second time I experienced the power of real estate, but this time not in a Buy-Fix-Hold-Sell scenario but a Buy-Fix-Rent-Hold scenario. My message is have no fear because one can make money in any strategy but it requires time, knowledge and education, trial and error, a system and a network to find good deals. I'm living proof that, when you invest in yourself and surround yourself with an all-star team to do the heavy lifting for you, you're well on your way to success.

***

Laure's story makes it clear that you can always find good deals when you are clear on your objectives and motivated to act. She enjoys fixing up properties, so purchasing distressed buildings is something she's comfortable with. As she says, it is possible to make money with any strategy, so long as it fits your unique strengths and approach as an investor. Like all good investors and coaches, Laure emphasizes the wisdom of assembling a great team from the beginning to 'do the heavy lifting' involved in finding and purchasing good properties. This way you spend more of your time leveraging your strengths to create the maximum benefit for your business.

5 Pointers to Remember

In an article entitled *5 Ways to Know That You've Found a Great Investment Property*, Dave Peniuk of RevNYou.com offers a good pocket reference to help you know when a property is worth taking the plunge for. He and Julie make it clear both in this article and elsewhere that there really are no hard-and-fast rules about this, since what represents a good deal will always be determined by a person's unique objectives as an investor. The properties you buy must represent a good deal to you *personally*, so your real estate investment business can give you the life you want to have. That said, the tips that Dave shares here are still worth keeping handy.

The first point he mentions is to make sure the property meets your cash flow objectives using the Gross Rent Multiplier (GRM), which is the asking / purchase price divided by twelve times the monthly rent – it will ideally come out at 10 or lower. This will be important no matter where your property is located, but as always in real estate, location is king. Is the area thriving economically, creating a demand for housing? Are there clear improvement efforts underway on the part of government, citizens, or both (he and Julie use new Starbucks locations as indicators of this). He also encourages scouting out a good property manager or two even before you need one, since it's not always easy to secure one on short-notice. Finally, he speaks to the importance of keeping an eye on vacancy rates, since you may lose money buying properties in areas where the vacancy rate is 10% or higher.

While it's helpful to have guidelines like this, it's important to remember that list price doesn't necessarily have anything to do with a property's true value to *you*. What this means is that you need to make offers based on what seems like a good price to you, not to someone else. You know what you're willing and able to spend, and what other factors especially matter to you. By keeping your eye on the 'why' as you keep track of the details, you set yourself up to achieve success *as you define it* with real estate investment.

When you combine staying focused on your strengths with doing due diligence to discover true market value, you set yourself up to succeed. As a woman, your life experiences and innate qualities have given you an enhanced ability to find and take advantage of real estate deals that can help make your dreams a reality. All that remains is to educate yourself, build your network, and ACT!

The Importance of a Support Group

On that note, I wish to conclude this chapter by reiterating the importance of surrounding yourself with plenty of 'cheerleaders' whose support will keep you going when things get tough. I love the way Dave Peniuk says it here:

I have yet to find one successful real estate investor that doesn't have a good support group or network around them. This goes beyond your realtors, brokers, insurance agents, accountants, etc. This is the someone or some people who are there when you need them most. They give you that push or helping hand when your persistence, hustle, and guts are on empty. This could be a spouse, friend, investing partner, business partner, parent, child, or even mentor. This is one of the reasons we always suggest investors join real estate investing clubs or start investing with a like-minded individual. You will not only learn a great deal from that support person, but you can also look to them for help or guidance when you struggle.

If, after reading this book, you feel the real estate investment bug beginning to bite, I want to assure you that I would be honoured to be that person for you. It's my passion to pool my resources with like-minded women who are ready to take their lives to the next level. Please get in touch when you're ready to explore the possibilities – I'll be thrilled to hear from you.

Chapter 7
Guaranteed Goals

The secret of success is constancy of purpose.
— Benjamin Disraeli

Dare to Live

There are many ways to set and achieve goals, but there is one that puts all others to shame. It's simple, clean and it's guaranteed to work better than any other system you could use. That's why we're going to call this system **Guaranteed Goals** and we're going to dare you to live!

If you'll only follow all the steps, then I can guarantee them. The truth is there is only one thing that can stop anyone from achieving their goals—and that is time. We're all going to die sometime, but until that happens there's nothing to stop us in the pursuit of our dreams.

Where did the system originate? I was told that back in the days of the Robber Barons, of the big steel companies and such, a young man came into the office of an important man. He wasted no time and came straight to the point. He would like to give the man a system for getting more done than could be done by any other system there was. He asked for no fee, saying that the man should keep the system and use it until he was satisfied it was as useful as he had been told. At that point, if he was so inclined, he could send the young man a cheque for whatever he felt the information was worth. A few months later the young man received a $25,000 check in the mail. What was that system? Read on …

The System:

1. Take a blank sheet of paper, putting aside an hour for this task, and write down every single goal you want to achieve in your life; no goal is too great, and no goal is too small. Do not stop (no matter how hard it gets) until the hour is up. Include all the following categories: work, play, family, health, spirit and wealth.

2. Prioritize the goals you've written down for each category. The classification will be (in descending order of importance): important and urgent, urgent but not important, important but not urgent, and neither important nor urgent.

3. Take the most important goal from each category and break it down into its component pieces. Don't worry if you don't get all of the pieces, you'll add them in when it's time for them. Now, take the most urgent and important task from each group and put it on your to-do list for tomorrow.

4. You should now have an urgent/important task you can do for each of the groups I mentioned. Reprioritize this new, balanced to-do list using the same criteria as in step number two. Tomorrow, go to work on your number one goal. Throw heart and soul into it. If interrupted, deal with the situation, and then happily go back to work on your goal. Give no thought or worry to the other goals on your list until you finish number one.

5. When finished your number one goal, move to your number two goal, once again throwing heart and soul into the effort. Repeat until your list is done or you reach the end of the day. Before you go to bed, go through steps three to four and build a new list. Items from the previous day will normally roll over to the new day (sometimes an urgent and important task will supercede and rise to the top of your list).

Do the steps as laid out for you and you'll find you'll be getting more of what you want done, you'll feel happier doing these things and you'll get more done than any other method you've tried. You'll know your guaranteed goals will get done—if you maintain this ongoing **awareness** you've been given; if you take the massive action I'm suggesting; if you pay **attention** to the results you're getting or not getting (**analysis**); and if you change your approach as necessary (**adjustment**). Yes, you can achieve your guaranteed goals if you'll only use the steps laid out and the success system that followed. I call it the **Four A's of Achievement.**

But you don't have to stop there. You can take out some insurance. You can borrow the following system that helps you bridge the gap between what you are capable doing and what you are willing to do. It's called *60 Seconds to Success* and was developed by long-time author, Clayton Clifford Bye. The simple techniques will give you the ability to replace limiting patterns of behaviour with sets more likely to produce to the results you want. Once this system is learned, there should be nothing standing between you and success that practice and vigilance won't remove ...

60 Seconds to Success

There are no limitations to the mind except those we acknowledge.
– Napoleon Hill

The central idea presented in *60 Seconds to Success* is that it only takes a minute to change your behaviour. No matter what the situation may be—you have the ability to choose what you think, feel, say or do. You determine the results you get from life, not your wife, not your husband, not your friends, not your boss or any of the countless other people or events you'll encounter throughout your life. Make a better choice in this moment; your rewards <u>will</u> be greater in the next. Do this consistently, and you've changed your life.

The system is composed of four parts that you have already been given: awareness, action, analysis and adjustment. Become *aware* of what you have to do, take *action* on a massive scale, *analyze* your results and make whatever *adjustments* your results indicate. All these things can be done on a daily basis and take just moments to initiate; hence the term *60 Seconds to Success.*

The key to the entire system is the technique of changing your attitude (the sum total of your thoughts, feelings, words and actions) through the asking and answering of specific questions. Questions determine your perspective, your point of view, your judgement, the very meaning of your experiences.

We witness an event. The questions we ask about that experience give it meaning and definition. Our ensuing thoughts, emotions, words and actions are then influenced by this perspective. The pattern of behaviour that follows is our attitude.

To explain it in a slightly different way: Questions and answers form the structure of your inner conversations. Your inner conversations influence how you perceive what happens to you and, ultimately, determine the pattern of your actions.

The point of all this discussion? If you're to succeed in life, you must cause the results you want. That means consciously generating (or causing) thoughts, emotions, words and actions that have specific meanings and purposes. The humble question is the right tool for the job.

I believe that every successful person shares one ability: They're able to visualize the things they want with absolute clarity, seeing events as if they've already happened, creating an intense vision of the future that compels them to action (and according to Raymond may actually draw the Universe toward themselves). The absolute certainty these individuals have (that they can achieve what they've set out to do) becomes the burning desire Napoleon Hill wrote about in his book, *Think and Grow Rich*.

Know what you want! Get excited about it. Visualize it happening. Make it the first thing you see when you get out of bed in the morning and the last thing you concentrate on before going to bed at night. Think about your dream every chance you get. Make it your passion, your desire, your magnificent obsession. Create a vision that fills you with excitement, enthusiasm and energy—you'll get what you want from life.

Question:

What, specifically, do you want from life? Put these goals on paper. Make your answers clear enough that you're able to call up the images involved at will. Paint vivid pictures with your words. Get excited! Make the list now.

Spend at least 15 minutes every day clarifying this vision of the future. Write down new details. Create a blueprint of this dream you're chasing. Give it no chance to slip away.

What you do on a daily basis makes all the difference in life. The completion of many small tasks with a specific goal in mind — the process of taking consistent and purposeful action — leads to massive results over the long run. Concentrate on what you can do, not on what you can't. Train yourself to think in terms of "I want to do this," or "I like doing this." Eliminate the phrases "I have to, I must, I can't." Become a "happy action-taker." Practice doing the things you want to become good at, that you'll enjoy doing. Practice, practice, practice.

Questions:

What tasks are to be performed, and which resources are needed, in order to make this dream of yours happen? Prioritize these requirements. Set time limits for achieving them. Break the goals down into simple components or individual tasks.

Which of the simplified tasks you listed can you do, right now? Record the task, then do it.

Finish one job and move onto another. Work through your list of goals, by order of importance. Don't think about how many jobs there are, or whether or not you can get them done. Take one task at a time. Record it, do it and go on to the next.

At the end of the day, note your accomplishments, allow yourself to feel good about what you've done, then ask "What tasks will I do tomorrow?"

Set aside time to prioritize and plan each day's events. Make sure the bulk of your activities are designed to move you toward your goals.

Develop the ability to notice what's working and what's not. Keep a daily activity journal. Record your results honestly. Take responsibility for your successes and your failures. Use this written record to keep you moving toward your goals at all times.

Questions:

Did the behaviours you chose today produce the intended results? If not, why not?

What could you have done to avoid these less than perfect results?

What can you do in the future to keep this from happening again?

Practice doing quick evaluations of your actions as you perform them. What's going well? What can you do to you improve on this? If the results you desire aren't materializing, what can you do differently? How can you make this situation work for you?

Record your observations in your journal. Construct a plan to avoid similar (undesirable) results in the future.

When something doesn't work, change your approach. Try something different. Be a Contrarian, and consider the opposite of what everyone else is doing. Better yet, find someone who's already done what you want to do and emulate them. Truly successful people are so few and far between—they had to have done something unique, don't you agree?

Questions:

Where are the opportunities in your current situation?

How can your recent mistakes or failures work for you?

What's good about the problems you're presently working on?

What can you learn from your recent mistakes or failures?

What can you do, right now and with respect to your current problems, that will move you closer to your goals—in a way that will allow you to enjoy yourself?

Attitude is a description of you in relation to your current situation. It's the sum total of all your thoughts, feelings, words and actions. Change your attitude, right now, and you'll change the results you're getting, right now. You won't find a simpler recipe for taking control of your life than that!

Questions:

What single thought will you choose today to help you move you toward your goals?

What specific feeling can you cultivate today to help support you while you pursue your goals?

What phrase and/or action will you use to bring your dreams closer to reality?

Make a list of questions you can use in tough situations to drive limiting thoughts from your mind. Use these questions to focus your thoughts on your goals, rather than on who's to blame or the countless other destructive thoughts that can be elicited by unexpected events.

An example question would be "How can I make this situation work for me?"

Come up with at least three more questions you can use to focus your thoughts in difficult times:

Choose some similar questions for emotions, words and actions (at least three questions for each).

Ask questions like "What's good about this situation? What reasons do I have for feeling enthusiastic or excited or successful? What do I have to feel grateful for? Is there anything I can say that will move me closer to my goals? What can I do differently that will move me closer to my goals?"

Identify questions that cause empowering answers to flood into your brain instead of the defeatist, paralyzing, useless crap that permeates our society!

Most people spend their lives trying to avoid problems, dealing with them only when forced to—and then with trepidation. Is this a wise approach? After all, the only people who don't have problems are dead people. Wouldn't your time be better spent learning how to profit from the problems you encounter?

Questions:

Failure (the achievement of results other than those we want) is the way we learn. It's an integral part of success. What have you learned from your most recent failure?

Problems are the guardians of all of life's treasures. Have you found the treasure hiding at the core of your largest and most recent problem? If not, how can you make this problem work for you?

Every problem can be dealt with in the same manner:

1. What is the problem? Be exact.
2. What are all the possible solutions?
3. Which of these is the best solution?
4. Devise a plan (a series of tasks) to achieve this solution.
5. Act on your plan.
6. If there's no solution available to you, adjust your attitude so as to minimize the mental, emotional and physical impact of the problem. Get on with your life.

Decision making is about taking action. The process involves making the best choice possible, acting on it, then evaluating the results achieved.

There's a method of decision making I've used for years. The only time the technique ever failed me is when I failed to use it!

The Ben Franklin Method:

Take a blank sheet of paper. Write the decision you must make across the top of it. Now, draw a line down the center of the remaining blank area. On the left side, write down all the reasons you have for going ahead with the course of action being considered. On the right side write down all the reasons you have for not proceeding. Tally up the pros and cons, then go with whichever course of action has the highest total. You can give one point for each reason listed, or you can weight them according to impact or significance. Just be honest in your assessment.

I was a long time discovering this next point: *Your earnings in life will correspond exactly to the level of service you provide to others.* We're paid for the value we provide—and for nothing else. If I have a million dollars and you have something to offer me which I consider to possess the value of a million dollars (and I have either the need or want of it), you have within your grasp a million dollars!

Baseball players don't earn million-dollar salaries because their talent is worth that much. They earn such big bucks because you and I place high value on entertainment. If we weren't prepared to pay exorbitant fees to be entertained in this manner (or advertisers weren't willing to pay huge fees to access us while we're being entertained), the players wouldn't earn exorbitant wages. Supply and demand is based on the concept of VALUE.

Questions:

What can you do today to increase the value you provide to your employer, your customers, your spouse, your community? Don't continue until you've come up with something in each area.

Spend at least 15 minutes per day—with a blank sheet of paper and a pencil—looking for ways to provide more value in your job and your life.

What could stand improvement ...
a) in your place of business?
b) in your personal life?
c) in your community?

What idea, service or product can you come up with to rectify each of these problems, and who would value your offering the most? Devise a plan to go out and sell these ideas!

You can motivate yourself. It's easy to do. There are two reasons why anyone does anything: To avoid pain and to gain pleasure. We're either moving toward something we want, or we're moving away from something we don't want.

For example: When you do something unpleasant or painful, it's because you expect to gain something—in the long run—that's pleasurable enough to compensate for your pain. Studying to become a doctor or working at a job you hate in order to pay for your dream home are a couple of things that come to mind.

High achievers are people who take action in all circumstances. They do this because they know that greater rewards will be earned in the long run. They've given themselves enough good reasons to pursue their dreams that they're compelled to action. And that's the secret: You can overcome the many faces of fear and reach high levels of motivation just by giving yourself enough good reasons to act!

Exercise:

Write down three pleasurable things you expect to gain when you adopt the techniques offered in 60 SECONDS TO SUCCESS.

Write down three painful (or unpleasant) things you expect to avoid when you adopt the techniques offered in 60 SECONDS TO SUCCESS.

Come up with at least two new reasons every day for feeling excited, enthusiastic and energetic about the future. Write these things down and review the entire list every morning. Keep at it until you have 60 reasons for taking action on a daily basis. You'll be motivated! *I was.*

Write down the first two questions now.
Come up with at least two good motivational questions you can ask yourself every morning when you wake up.
(Hint: These questions should inspire positive emotions that get you taking immediate action.)

POWER QUESTIONS

1. Will this behaviour help me get what I want?

   a) Are these thoughts helping me get what I want from life?

   b) Are these feelings going to help me move closer to my goals?

   c) If I say this, will I move closer to my goals?

   d) Will this action produce results that will help me get what I want from life?

   e) What pleasant results will I experience if I go ahead with this behaviour?

   f) What unpleasant results will I experience if I go ahead with this behaviour?

   g) Are these the results I really want?

2. What can I do, right now, that will move me closer to my goals?

   a) What reasons do I have for doing this; what pleasant

results will I experience, and what unpleasant results will I avoid?

3. What am I doing that isn't perfect yet, and what can I do to improve my results?

4. What could I have done to prevent this situation/event?

5. What can I do to keep it from ever happening again?

6. What have I got to be grateful for?

7. What's good about this situation?

8. How can I make this problem work for me?

9. Where's the opportunity in this situation?

The above questions are designed to focus your thoughts on what you can do instead of what you can't do. The questions can also get you taking actions more likely to move you in the direction of your goals. Pick your answers carefully. Cultivate the thoughts, feelings, words and actions most likely to get you what you want from life. Eliminate all else.

Come up with your own list of power questions. Keep adding to it (and amending it) until you end up with a set of questions you'll use on a daily basis. Ask these questions every chance you get—and watch your life change!

It takes but a minute to change your behaviour and, thus, the results you get from life. The following daily recipe helps you put your focus on producing behaviours and results that move you toward the future you want. The reasoning is simple: If you consistently move toward a specific destination, you must eventually reach it.

Begin Your Voyage to Success Today!

1. Waking up:
Start each day with questions designed to get you excited, enthusiastic and energized.
Example: What can I do, right now, that will make me feel excited, enthusiastic and that will get me moving with the energy of a peak performer? Do it!

2. Taking action:
Action creates emotion. Anytime you falter, ask the question "What can I do, right now, that will allow me to enjoy myself and pursue goals?" Do it! (I always refer to my prioritized list of goals when I ask this question.)

3. Creating focus:
Target something you're thinking about, feeling, saying or doing at this moment. Is this behaviour moving you closer to your goals? If not, what thoughts, feelings, words or actions can you choose that will move you in the direction you want to go? Do these things!

Repeat step 3 on a regular basis throughout the day, especially when switching tasks, making decisions or choosing a course of action.

4. Free time activities:
a) Still have lots of energy? Check your goal/priority lists for work, play, education, spiritual development—whatever: What task tops the list you selected? Do it!

b) Need to add to your list of things to do? Want to work on something different? Identify a problem related to your goals:
- What's the problem?
- What are all the possible solutions?
- What's the best one?
- How can you get from where you are now to the place where this solution has taken place? List these tasks and prioritize them.
- Do the first task on the list. Now!

c) Want to sit for awhile? Brainstorm:

- Describe one of your current problems in a single sentence. Record this statement at the top of a blank sheet of paper.

- Write down everything you can think of that could help you solve the problem. No idea is too dumb.

- Keep at it for at least 15 minutes.

- Highlight the best ideas for future use.

d) Feeling lethargic? Need some motivation? Develop some reasons for action:

- Using either the Ben Franklin Method or the brainstorming method just described, select some tasks you want to accomplish and list reasons for following through. Hint: People do things for only two reasons—to avoid pain or to gain pleasure.

5. Turning in:

- Before going to bed, make a list of tasks for tomorrow.

- Prioritize these goals, and make a promise to yourself to complete each in order of importance.

- Prepare your morning questions.

Put your focus on results, and never look away. You'll get what you want from life. I know you will.

Chapter 8
The Six MAINLY® Pathways of Life

If you want to keep getting what you are getting,
just keep doing what you've been doing.
– Unknown

Dare to Choose

There are six pathways of life that form an acronym: MAINLY®. Raymond has used these in his life and for his thousands of mentored clients around the world. These pathways form the basis of monthly and annual planning and are so different from anything else you will have seen that I feel they belong in this book.

The six MAINLY® pathways of life are:

MESS	Choose to clean a Mess each month.
ACKNOWLEDGMENT	Choose to express gratitude each month.

INCREASE IN WEALTH   Choose to improve your financial situation each month.

NEW   Choose to do something new each month.

LEARN   Choose to learn something each month.

YOURSELF   Choose to do something just for yourself each month.

When you set a goal in each one of the six pathways mentioned above and you achieve a Minimum Level™ of success in each one, some amazing things will happen:

1. You will find yourself striding confidently forward in your life.
2. You will find yourself following a holistic vision.
3. You will find yourself improving *synergistically*, with all aspects of your life helping other aspects.
4. Your life becomes more whole.

Note: It is important to investigate and clearly understand each pathway.

Choose to Clean a Mess Each Month

A *Mess* is any situation in which what is outside of you is not equal to what is inside of you. In other words, it is any situation in which what you've got is not what you really want. It is an *incongruence* in your life. It is any negative, uncomfortable situation, physical thing, relationship or aspect of your environment that you are *tolerating*.

Messes rob you of vitality. They teach you that you can't handle tasks. They laugh at you. Messes make you cringe. They make you apologize to others. Messes diminish you. They do not merely belittle you; they actually have a major impact on your financial well-being.

Raymond has observed that wealthy people tend to be orderly, while those who struggle have lots of messes. In fact it is the ones who *first* clean their messes who *then* become wealthy. Fundamentally: Each mess is a lock on the gate that keeps abundance out. And every mess you eliminate, *no matter how small,* brings relief of enormous proportions.

Take a blank piece of paper, entitle it "Messes I wish to one day clean." Stay with it until you have at least 25 messes on your list from all aspects of your life. You'll find the most important messes will show up on that list from many different parts of your life. Pick one from work, relationships, money, health, spirit and play—for example—and add them to your short- to medium-term goals.

Choose to Express Gratitude Each Month

Everything that goes up must come down. You are refreshed in the morning and then tired at night. You are young and then you are old. Trees grow tall and then fall over. The tide is high and then the tide ebbs. This is the inescapable cycle of life. In fact your life can be full or it can be empty; it's all about how you look at the word gratitude.

The cure for a life of emptiness is a life of gratitude. Stated differently, emptiness is simply unbalanced depreciation or consuming without gratitude. So the answer for the wealthy, for example, who feel unfulfilled is for them to express their appreciation to the same extent that they are involved in spending.

Let's look at it this way: if you choose to give back rather than taking from the world, you are choosing to express gratitude. If you volunteer to help build a House for Habitat rather than buying a new car, you are expressing gratitude. A simple thank you for being alive may make you feel good for a moment or two, but an action that counters what you take from the world (think of everything you buy) will make you feel great for a long time. Ask anyone who has every participated in a charity or who made something new from what they took from the world.

This formula also works in reverse. If your income is lower than your gratitude, then increasing your gratitude will cause your income to rise to balance your level of gratitude. And, if your income is higher than your gratitude, then increasing your gratitude will produce joy, not emptiness.

At the age of 18, I made up my mind to never have another bad day in my life. I dove into a endless sea of gratitude from which I've never emerged.
—Patch Adams

Choose to Improve Your Financial Situation Each Month

Most people think of investing when they see the above pathway, but investing is just a small part of what you can do to improve your financial situation. For example, you can:
- Reduce your debts
- Create a financial plan
- Increase your sales
- Get more clients
- Network
- Advertise
- Get a credit card
- Get rid of a credit card

- Pay off the balance on a credit card
- Raise your fees or your prices
- Get a raise if you are employed
- Buy a piece of real estate
- Buy stocks or mutual funds
- Improve your referral system
- Increase your savings account
- Mortgage a property
- Pay down a mortgage
- Decrease the interest rate on your debt
- Increase the interest on your savings
- Sell something you own

Basically, to impact your financial situation in a positive way you can:
- Increase your assets
- Increase your income
- Decrease your debts
- Decrease your expenses

If you do not consciously improve your financial situation every month, in some way, then the years slip by. A sailboat with no rudder ends up wherever the wind happens to blow.

You can powerfully bolster your financial situation by making regular, consistent improvements, even of a minor nature, each month. And this approach is guaranteed, without any magic potions. Make a financial step, even a small one, every month, and you will win.

In fact, I'll let you in on one of the most powerful secret of them all: by making regular, consistent improvements – even of a minor nature, each month, to each of the major aspects of your life (health, spirit, family, work, play and wealth) you can transform that life beyond your wildest dreams.

Choose to Do Something New Each Month

"The only thing constant is change," said Heraclitus some 2,500 years ago. And it's even more true today. Our world is changing at a rate never seen before. If you are standing still, trying to maintain your place in the world, then you are actually slipping backwards. By choosing to do something new each month you can change this. Otherwise you face the prospect of your world collapsing inward on you.

In business you could:
- Develop a new product or service
- Improve an existing product or service
- Get a new computer software program. to allow you to do something new
- Create a website

- Offer something new to a client
- Advertise in a new way
- Offer a contest or some special new. inducement to your clients, and so on

In your personal life it could be:
- Try a different type of restaurant
- Meet new people
- Read a new book
- Read a magazine that you would not normally buy
- Update your wardrobe
- Try a new hairstyle
- Have some new experience
- Join a club
- Begin participating in a new sport
- Go somewhere new, and so on

This may not seem like an earth-shattering plan, but you can be assured that some of your new experiences will be a big hit in your life. Besides, relentless pursuit of a path that investigates something new each month will open your horizons, broaden your scope of options, allow different people to enter your life, eliminate fixed thinking, and in many other ways open you up to the exciting diversity that surrounds you. Be warned, however; this is not an easy thing to continue to do. Have someone in your corner rooting for you. This could be a good friend, a co-worker, a mentor or even a mastermind group.

Choose to Learn Something Each Month

You can never keep up with the mind-boggling explosion of knowledge (in every field of discipline) that the invention of the microchip has wrought upon this world. However, you can increase your knowledge every month in some way. That is enough to make major changes in your own life.

- become more skilled in a certain area
- take a course
- learn a new computer program
- learn a new personal skill
- read a non-fiction book
- watch the Biography or the History Channel
- take a personal growth course
- learn about a new hobby or sport
- learn how to use your camera or your computer better, and so on

Why should you be concerned enough to take on yet another challenge? Doctors are making less money because they know less and less every month and patients are learning more and more every month. Bookkeepers have largely been replaced by computer programs. The ATM machine has bank tellers struggling to maintain their jobs and even Lawyers are making less, because you can get what they used to charge money for online or from a computer program. The list goes on and on, but you don't have to be on it.

Choose to Do Something Just For Yourself Each Month

Whatever your purpose in life is, you should enjoy yourself as you are pursuing it. Doing something for you is taking care of yourself. It is treating yourself in some way that is important and enjoyable to you. Here are some examples:

- eliminate an addiction
- begin an exercise program
- lose weight
- reduce fats and sugars from your diet
- attend a special event
- fulfill a childhood dream
- have fun in some particular way you enjoy
- read a great book
- go on vacation
- spend time with special people
- go on a spiritual quest
- meditate
- visit someplace you want to see again
- play your favorite sport more often

Such times as these refresh, rebuild and renew. They will give you the heart to face your daily challenges. They will help to make your life the joy it should be.

And now ... three expert steps that will help you bring what you have just read into play in your life.

Expert action step one: Record any 10 goals and identify to which goal pathway they belong.

Expert action step two: Select one goal for this month in each of the six goal pathways (sound familiar?).

Expert action step three: Select at least three more goals in each of the six pathways (these comprise a warehouse for future months).

Chapter 9
Recording Goals so That They Achieve Themselves Automatically

Our life is what our thoughts make it.
– Marcus Aurelius

This chapter is about how you can employ the Law of Attraction to achieve your own goals, seemingly effortlessly. It is adapted from the writings of Raymond Aaron.

Pick the three most important results you want to accomplish this month. These are going to be big goals and listing them accomplishes two things. First, it alerts the Universe to begin activating the Law of Attraction on your behalf. When you record, with heart and emotion, when you really desire, then the Universe listens. Second, it provides an overview of the goals you have just recorded.

These desired results are like the horizon. You never get to the horizon, but you can see it and aim for it. Yet these goal still need to be specific, they need to have a detailed deadline and they must have a three-tiered, measurable level of achievement. A *minimum* acceptable level of achievement; your *target* level of achievement; and an *outrageous* level of achievement. Let's look at an example …

First, the statement of the goal written the old way. I commit to traveling to London, England on November 14 for a special two week seminar that takes place in the latter half of November.

Next, the statement of the same goal written the new way. I commit to traveling to London, England on November 14 for a special two week seminar that takes place in the latter half of November, by breaking it into the following three levels:

Minimum acceptable level of achievement (you can be counted on to achieve this): Look up the cost of my flight

Target level of achievement (this is a stretch): Plan for the trip, including clothes to bring, all booking dates, times and costs. This means flights, hotel rooms, car rental and meals. Plan leisure time activities, find directions to seminar location and, among other things what the total cost will be.

Outrageous level of achievement (this is the one that seems practically impossible to achieve): Earn enough extra money this month to pay for the trip.

This is called the **MTO** (noun): The Minimum, Target and Outrageous levels of a goal.

Or the **MTO** (verb): To subdivide a goal into its Minimum, Target and Outrageous levels.

It's not your job to do these goals, only to ensure that they get done (there is a difference). The big differentiator between the two is *delegation*. In other words, there is nothing stopping you from finding a person to help you achieve the goal you are focusing on. Hire someone. Ask a friend or neighbor to help, ask a relative or even barter with someone. Be creative.

The other reason is by simply writing down these goals you get both your unconscious mind and The Law of Attraction working on your goal—even the one that seems impossible.

There are three different ways to divide a goal into its three MTO levels.
1.   **The Nested Technique™**
2.   **The Graduated Technique™**
3.   **The Deadline Technique™**

The Nested Technique to MTO a Goal ...

Minimum Level: I will do 10 sales this month (I am confident I can achieve this based on my actual history)

Target Level: I will do 20 sales this month (this would be in addition to achieving the Minimum Target Level)

Outrageous Level: I will do 30 sales this month (this would be in addition to achieving both the Minimum and the Target Levels

The Graduated Technique to MTO a Goal...

Minimum Level: I will help Laura (Laura is the easiest to work with)

Target Level: I will help Michelle (It's tougher to find time to work with Michelle)

Outrageous Level: I will help James (You find it quite the challenge to work with James)

But ... if you help James, you have not helped Laura or Michelle. The goals are achieved independent of each other, so the work done is not accumulative as it was in the nested technique. This is a BIG DIFFERENCE.

The Deadline Technique to MTO a Goal ... (The least used technique, probably because it's so scary). So assuming you set these goal on July 1, then ...

Minimum Level: I will make my first sale by July 30

Target Level: I will make my first sale by July 15

Outrageous Level: I will make my first sale by July 5

The Six Goal-Recording Rules:

1. The Deadline Rule

You know goals must have a deadline, but I say that goals have to have the *right* deadline. "I will clean my garage by July 15." That's a specific, immovable goal that you won't mistakenly put on your birthday or in the middle of winter or that will allow you to wiggle of the hook. Somewhere between today and July 15 you must have to have the garage cleaned. That's it and that's all.

2. Measurable

You can't know if you've achieved your goal if it isn't measurable. That is a fact. It's better to be clear that you didn't get a goal rather than stating the goal in such a vague way that you can't tell if you achieved it or not. It's simple really: write your goal accurately so that at the end of the time period you can stand up and say, "I got it!" or "I didn't get it."

3. Brief

Do not tell a story when setting a goal. Goals must be brief. Basically, the briefer a goal is the better the chance is that it's a well-written goal. "I will call my dad by September 15." You can't break that down without changing stated goal, can you? That's a good goal!

4. The Goal Must Be The Intended Result

You might state a goal like "I will get a 10% raise." Problem. Not only is thinking about 10% extremely difficult, because it's a concept, not a thing, it isn't the final result. "I will get a raise to $55,000 a year by January 1." Now that's a goal you can sink your teeth into. It's something you can imagine!

5. Positive

If you want to be able to focus on something you need to express it in positive terms. Otherwise the mind has great difficulty dealing with it. For example, try the goal "Do not think about a pink elephant." No matter how hard you try you will find yourself thinking about a pink elephant. So, instead, reframe using a positively stated goal: "Think of a beautiful blue jay." Do this and you are almost certain not to think about the pink elephant.

6. The Dreaded Per

The problem with saying you want to do something per week or per month is that if you miss that goal, is if you fail once there's no way to recover for the rest of the period. For example: I say "I'm going to brush my teeth twice per day for an entire month." If I miss one brush on day 3, there's no recovering my goal for the rest of the month. I just plain didn't make my overall goal. I would have been far better off saying "I will brush my teeth 60 times this month." Now

I can recover from a one brush day.

Annual Backwards Goals

How you can move strategically toward realizing even your biggest goals? Where do you envision yourself at the end of the year? What will you have achieved? Who will you be? How do you ensure your monthly goals line up with your vision for the year?

Any goal you have set for the month is a tactical goal. Tactical relates to taking those short-term actions along the way that support the strategic end result.

Typically, strategic goals, strategic plans, strategic planning and strategic thinking are longer term. Are your tactical monthly goals lined up with your overall strategy as to where you want to be a year from now? Maybe they are, and maybe they're not. One way to make sure is by recording annual goals.

Writing Goals Backwards

You can trick your mind into thinking that you have actually achieved a long-term goal—just by writing it down as if it was done in the past. Your mind can't differentiate between what you tell it is true and what has actually happened. Tricking your mind into thinking you've done what you are just gearing up to do, will allow you to do it "again" this year, easier than what you did the first time around. So if your goal is to earn $100,000 by the end of this year, you'll be speaking of your previous success in accomplishing this.

In fact, Raymond suggests writing a letter from the past to someone close, noting the things you did to achieve the goal. Listing specific skills and such are even better. The more real you make it sound the greater your chances of success.

By writing this letter, some of your successes will actually achieve themselves effortlessly just because you set that wheel in motion. This is the Law of Attraction at work.

It wouldn't hurt to hedge your bets by finding out exactly how someone else made the same amount of money. How do you do this? By asking an individual who has done it and by writing down the specific steps they used in specific order. This is called an algorithm, a set of steps you can follow to replicate what someone has done before. The more specific the algorithm, the better it will work for you.

To continue on … the way to finish up with your backwards goals is to list them exactly the way you did your short term goals—except you write everything down as if you have already done it. You know you are listing goals you want to achieve this year, but you write them down in terms of what you did. It's better to be proud of your achievements than to be wondering if you will have any.

Please refer to *Double Your Income Doing What You Love* by Raymond Aaron for examples of this letter.

Conclusion

If you want to be great and successful, choose people who are great and successful and walk side by side with them.
– Ralph Waldo Emerson

By now, I hope you realize that the innate qualities that you possess as a woman position you well to create a fulfilling and thriving real estate investing business. Your ability as a woman to notice the details, keep focused on your goals, cut through the crap, and leverage your connections with others makes for a winning combination. When you combine all this with your natural talent for finding a great deal, you can become truly unstoppable.

If you decide you want to embark on this exciting new adventure, it is imperative that you surround yourself with the right people. Raymond and I agree with many other coaches that this is perhaps the single most influential factor that determines your success: no one can reach their full potential in this business on their own. However, the right connections can make your business not only financially successful but fulfilling on a personal level as well. I like this quote from Mark Twain on the importance of keeping good company:

Keep away from people who try to belittle your ambitions. Small people always do that, but the really great make you feel that you, too, can become great.

There will always be people who think you're crazy for getting involved in real estate, who just can't imagine why you would even consider it. They have the right to limit themselves, but that doesn't mean you have to. Sadly, the ranks of those who belittle your ambitions will often include friends and family, and this is why it can be especially helpful to hire a coach who can support you with their knowledge, perspective, and insight. A big part of their job is to help you believe in yourself, because no one else will believe in you more than you believe in yourself, and this is key to establishing credibility as an investor.

In the spirit of this kind of empowerment, Raymond and I wish to emphasize that we wrote this book because *we want to work with you to make your dreams a reality.* Because my work with Raymond and others has been so instrumental to my success, I actively seek ways to leverage my experience for the benefit of other women. I am also always seeking potential investment partners whose objectives match mine, and whose gifts, talents, and resources complement my own.

I want to support you on your journey because I know that no woman is an island – we all stand on the shoulders of others at one time or another in life. We are never alone, and I am here to help you begin to build a network of support that will ensure your success.

May this book lay the first stone in a strong foundation for your success, built from passion and hard work.

Tammy and Raymond